Chinese Modern New Technology Series

3D Printing

Edited by Li Chaodong

Translated by Xuemeng Angela Li

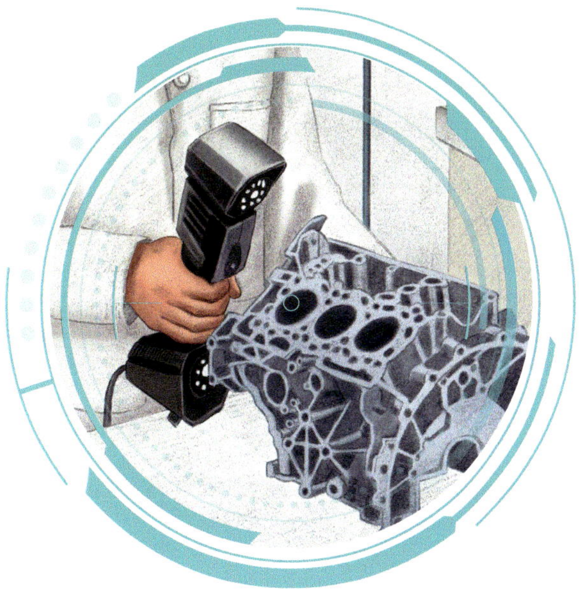

河海大學出版社
HOHAI UNIVERSITY PRESS

ROYAL COLLINS
Books Beyond Boundaries

Have you ever visited a factory?

There are many production lines in factories, where raw materials pass through to be processed in the machines and manufactured into standard products. This is the definition of standardization.

Under the mode of standardization, factories only need to prepare raw materials. Machines will automatically operate to continuously produce the same products repeatedly, saving labor costs and guaranteeing product quality.

Actually, standardization is not only applied in industrial production.

It has all played a role in everything from language and writing to textbooks and stationaries.

Standardization existed as early as the birth of human civilization, which can be seen in Cangjie's* creation of Chinese characters and Qin Shi Huang's (First Qin Emperor, 259–210 BC) unification of measures and weights.

Du (measuring instrument for length)

Heng (measuring instrument for weight)

Liang (measuring instrument for volume)

---

* A legendary ancient Chinese figure who invented Chinese characters.

Houmuwu *Ding*
Four-Goat Square *Zun*

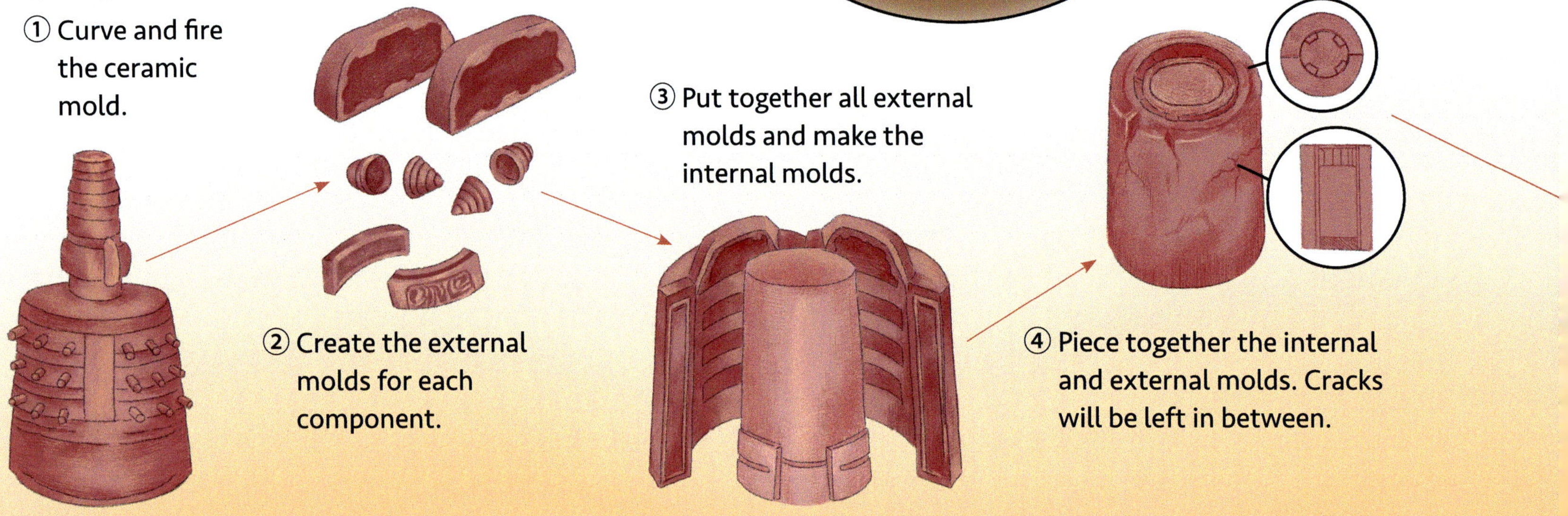
① Curve and fire the ceramic mold.
② Create the external molds for each component.
③ Put together all external molds and make the internal molds.
④ Piece together the internal and external molds. Cracks will be left in between.

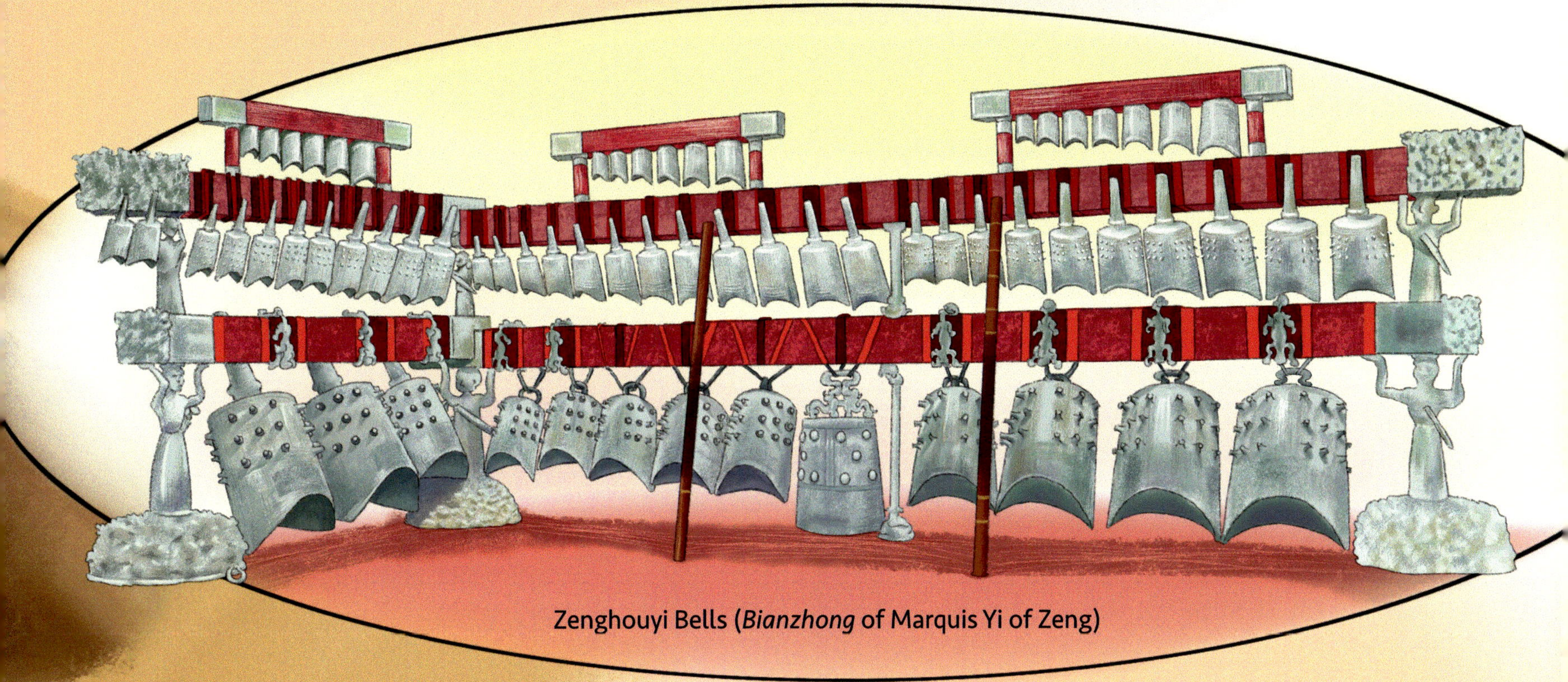

Zenghouyi Bells (*Bianzhong* of Marquis Yi of Zeng)

The bronze culture during the Shang and Zhou dynasties (1600–256 BC) was vigorous. At the time, any sacrificial event would easily take hundreds of bronze wares.

It is impossible to produce such great amounts of delicate bronze wares simply by relying on slow production with limited labor. That's how molds—the most important invention in the history of standardization—appeared.

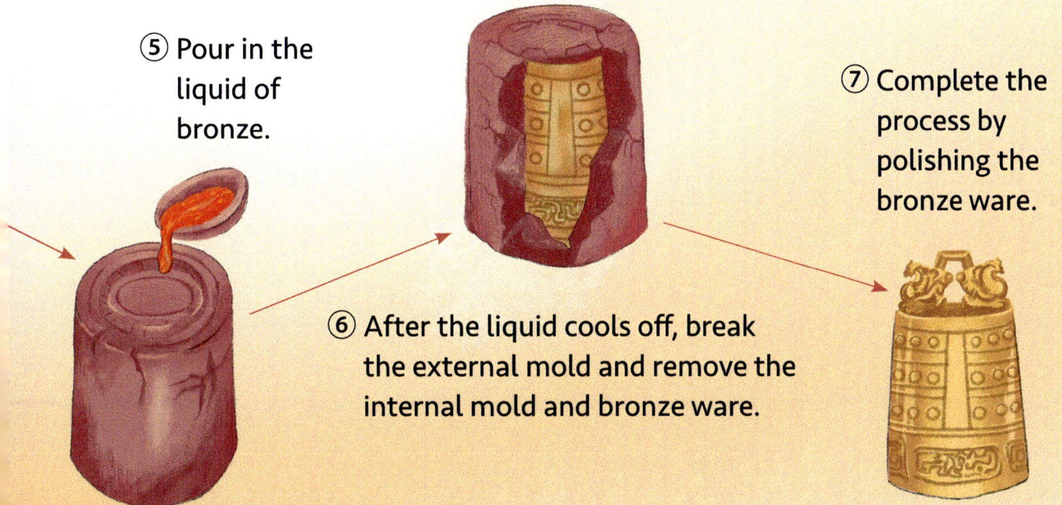

Mold was also known as the *fan* in ancient times. Ancient people used the *fan* and invented casting methods such as mold casting and lost-wax methods, which enabled the fast production of many bronze wares of similar sizes.

Initially, people need to break the external mold in order to take the bronze ware out. Later, they improved the method and created molds that can be recycled for repeated uses.

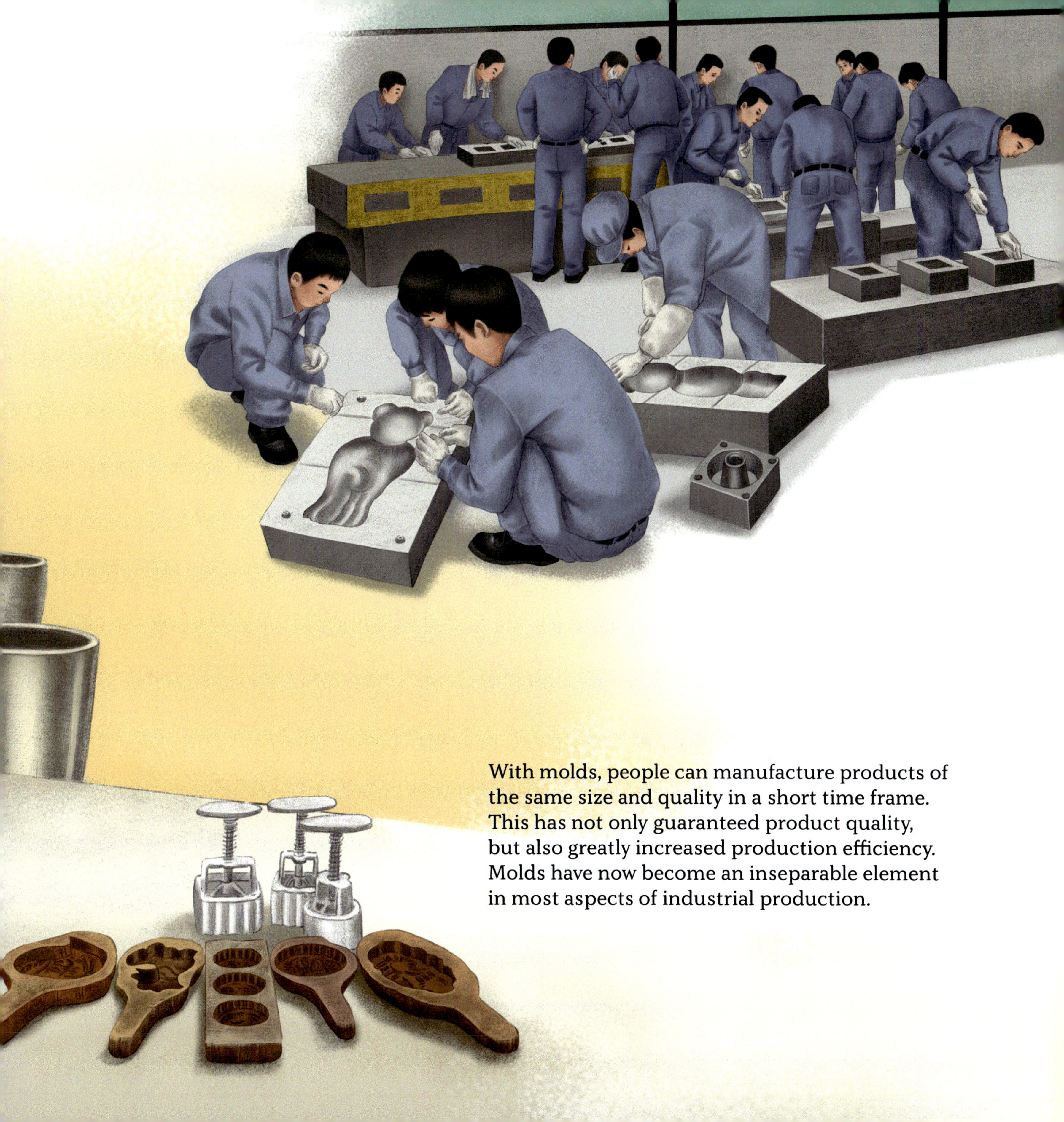

With molds, people can manufacture products of the same size and quality in a short time frame. This has not only guaranteed product quality, but also greatly increased production efficiency. Molds have now become an inseparable element in most aspects of industrial production.

The increase in the standardization level of industrial production goes hand in hand with an influential movement of the mid to late 18th century—the Industrial Revolution.

"Assembly Line" has been adopted in industrial production during this stage, in which every step requires the production to follow the established orders and rules. Assembly line production brought numerous products of reasonable price and high quality to people and marked the start of the rapid growth of human society.

With the increasingly close ties between each country, the standard of a single nation or industry can gradually transform into an international standard. Since the appearance of international standards, different regions and countries can work collaboratively by manufacturing individual components and putting them together into a complete product. Nowadays, most products are manufactured through such modes, ranging from phones to rockets.

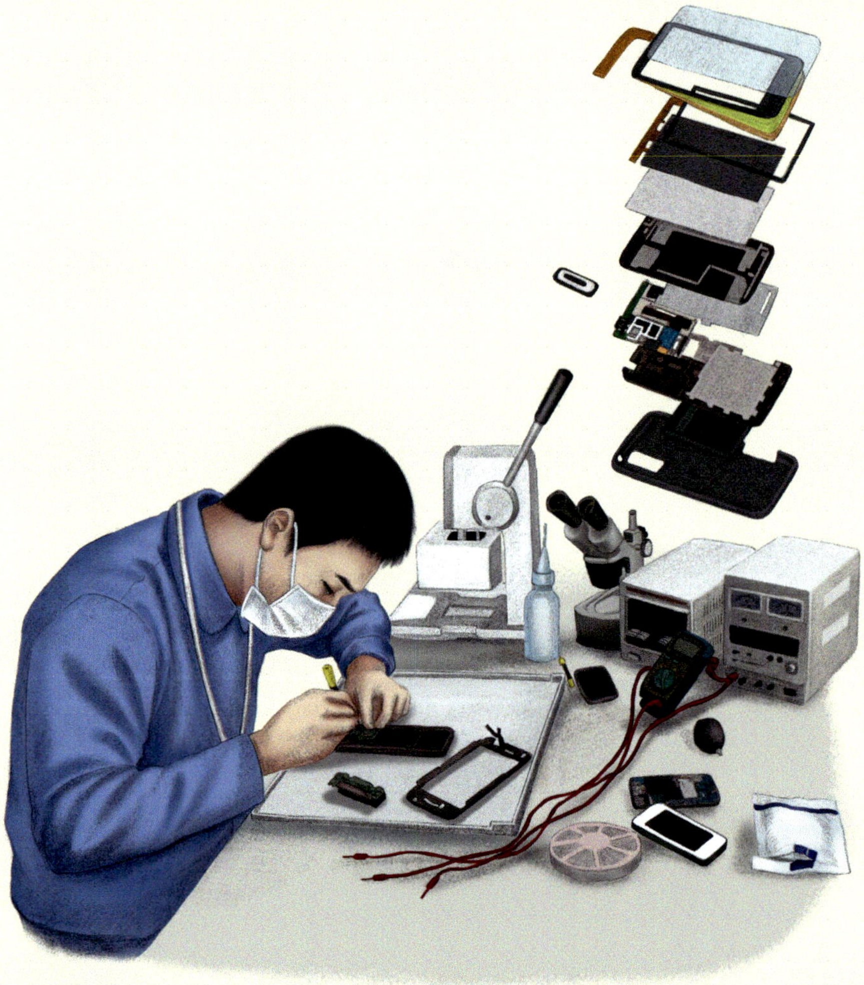

For instance, the completion of a modern airliner requires as many as three million components.

They are produced collaboratively by 1,500 companies from more than 30 countries around the world.

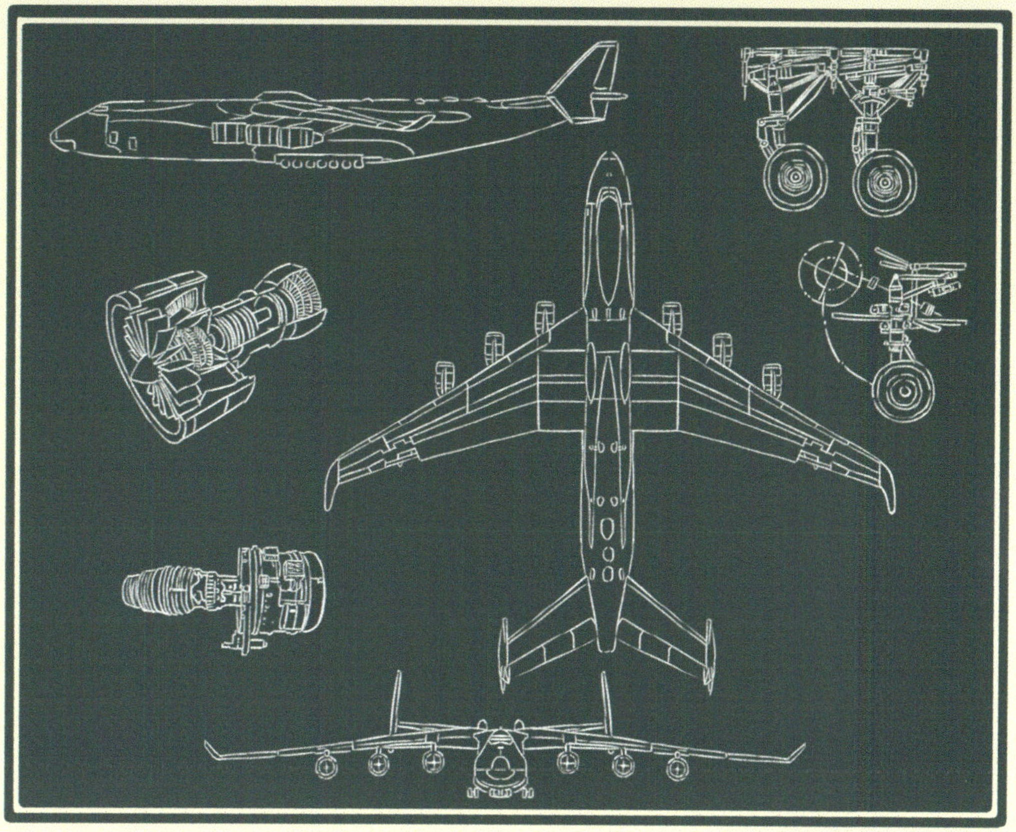

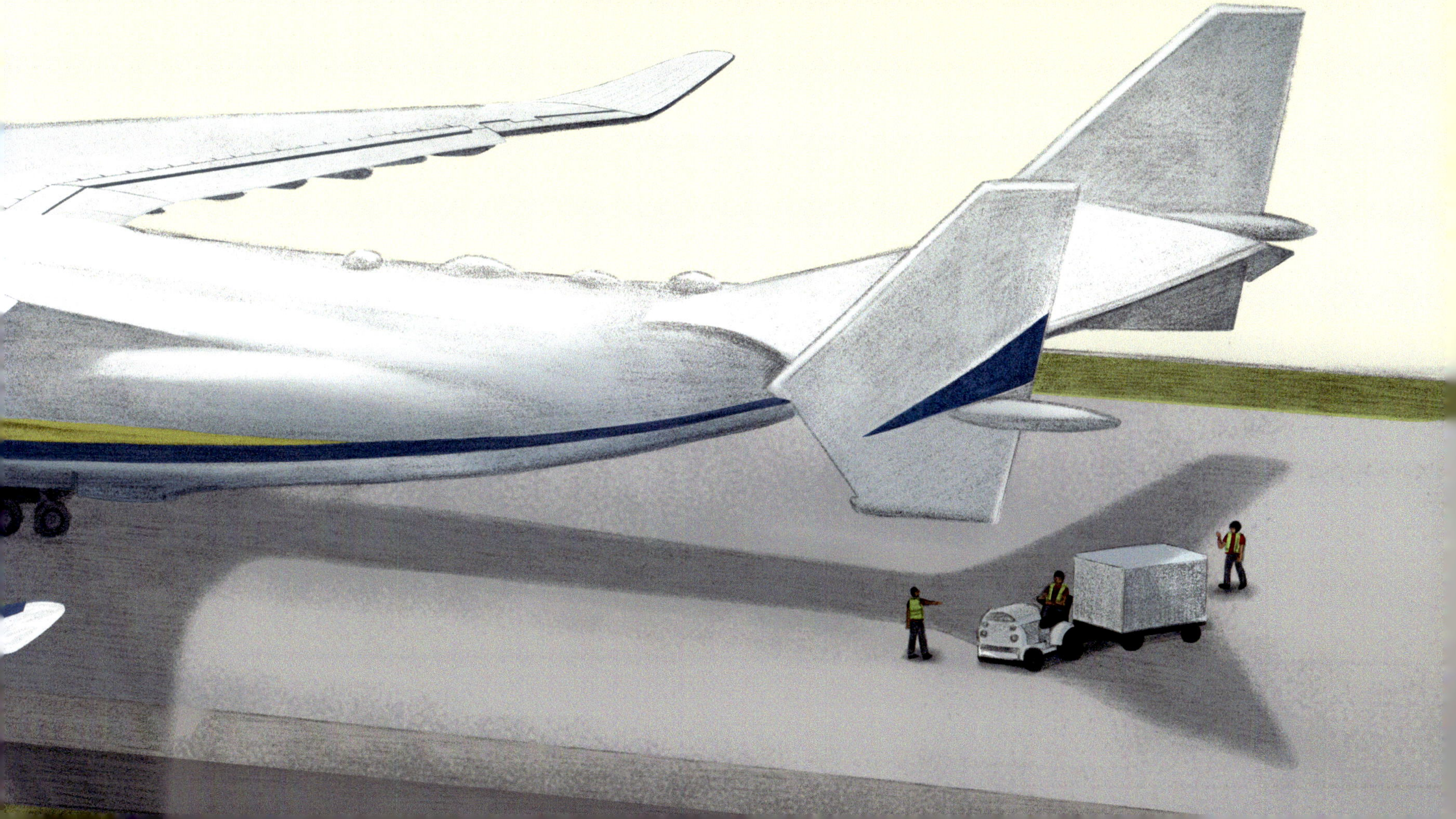

Zenghouyi *Zun-Pan*
(Bronze *Zun-Pan* Vessel of Marquis Yi of Zeng)

Although standardization boosts the efficiency of production, demands vary for each customer. People have been exploring the balance between standardization and personalization.

The world-renowned Terracotta Army of Qin Shi Huang is an experiment of such exploration during ancient times.

Terracotta Army is a part of the Mausoleum of the First Qin Emperor. Until now, about ten thousand pieces of terracotta army have been uncovered. However, each has distinctive details in its appearance, hairstyle, and clothes design. It can be said that every uncovered piece is a unique creation.

However, the cost of balancing standardization and personalization during the Qin Dynasty (221–207 BC) was extremely high. The firing of the terracotta army not only took many years, but also mobilized numerous civilians as laborers. It created an unbearable burden for the people of Qin and thus became the leading cause of the destruction of the state.

3D printing is the best example of combining personalization and standardization in modern society. The technology combines computer modeling and printing by first establishing models through computer programming and then printing out the complete model in reality with the robotic arm.

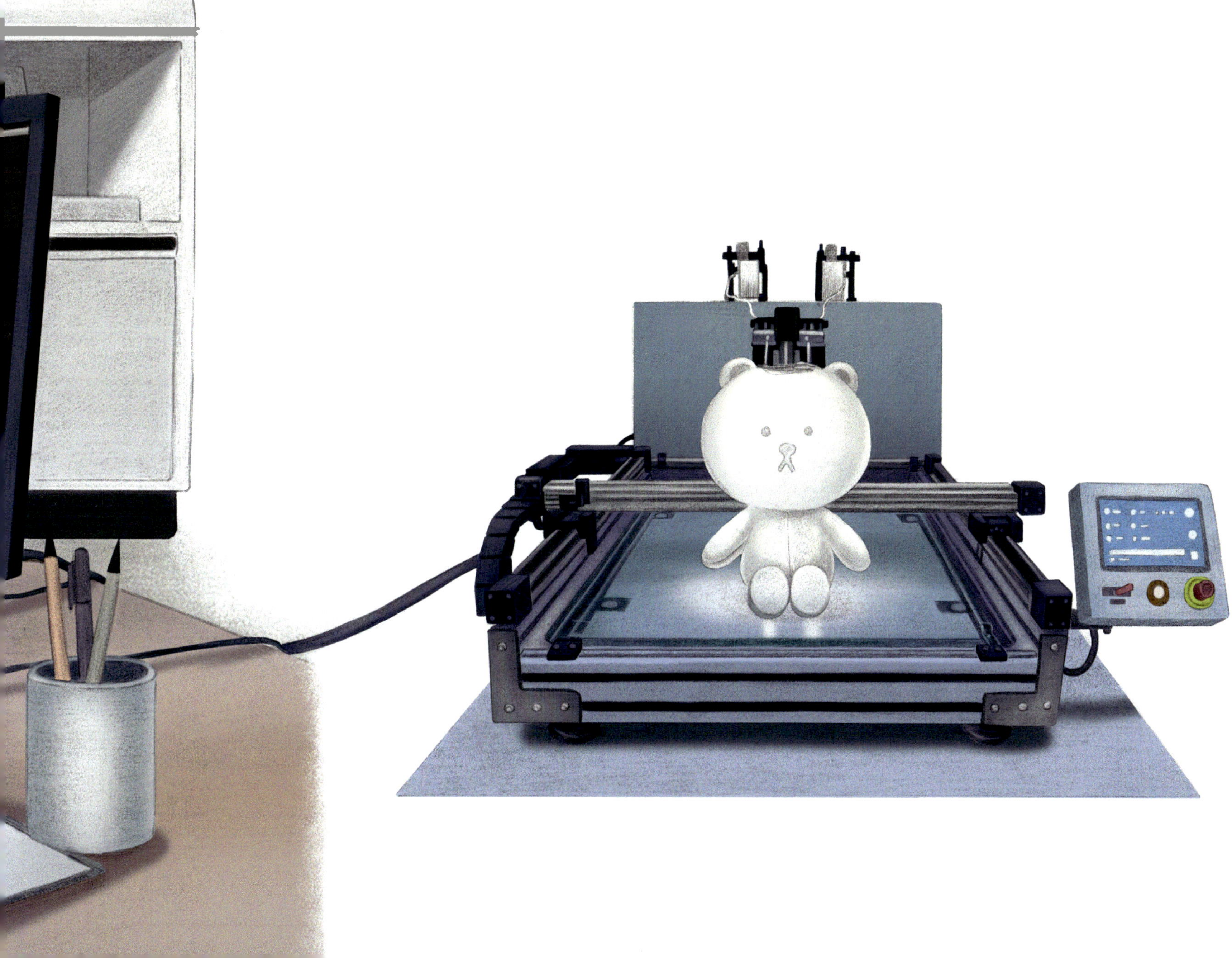

Based on the highly flexible models of computers, 3D printing has perfectly met the demands for personalization that traditional molds cannot satisfy. Its unique advantage comes with limitless potential.

There are various 3D printing shops online as well that take up the diverse printing needs of customers.

In healthcare, doctors can now customize appropriate human organs or medical devices according to the conditions of each patient to provide better treatment through 3D printing technology.

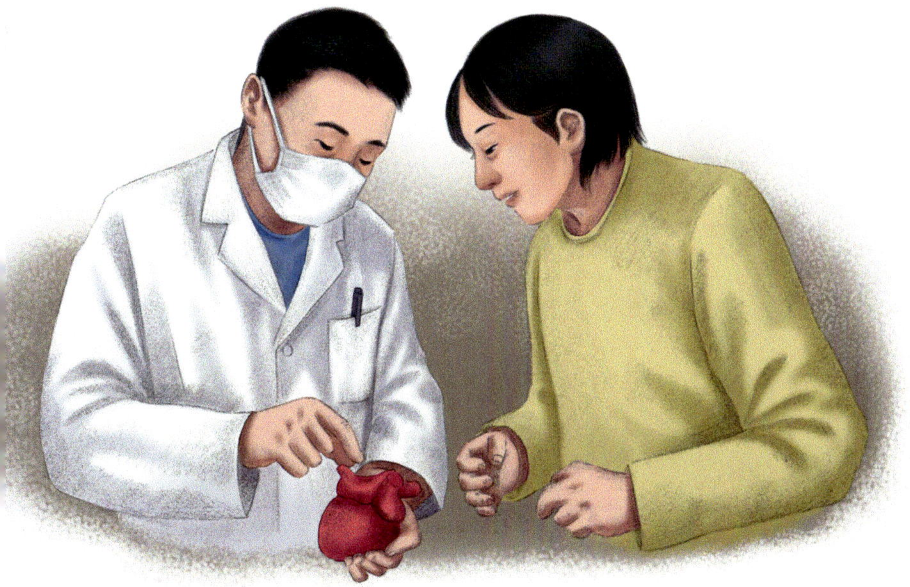

They can also scan and print out the surgery sites based on treatment needs when dealing with complicated surgeries. Doctors can then use the printed model as a real-life map to determine the best surgery plan.

In the architecture industry, to build a house, the construction itself already takes a significantly long period on top of initials steps, such as foundation laying and construction materials preparation.

The total time estimate from start to move-in can go up to several months if the interior finish is also counted.

However, if 3D printing technology is applied in the construction process, it only takes about 20 hours to build the house after establishing the model and setting up the devices. The printed house is instantly ready for move-in, offering a fast, environmentally friendly, and high-quality product.

To satisfy people's demands for detailed quality, laser technology is also applied in the process of 3D printing, which directly builds models through laser scans.

This method simplifies the steps of computer modeling and improves the productivity of the original method.

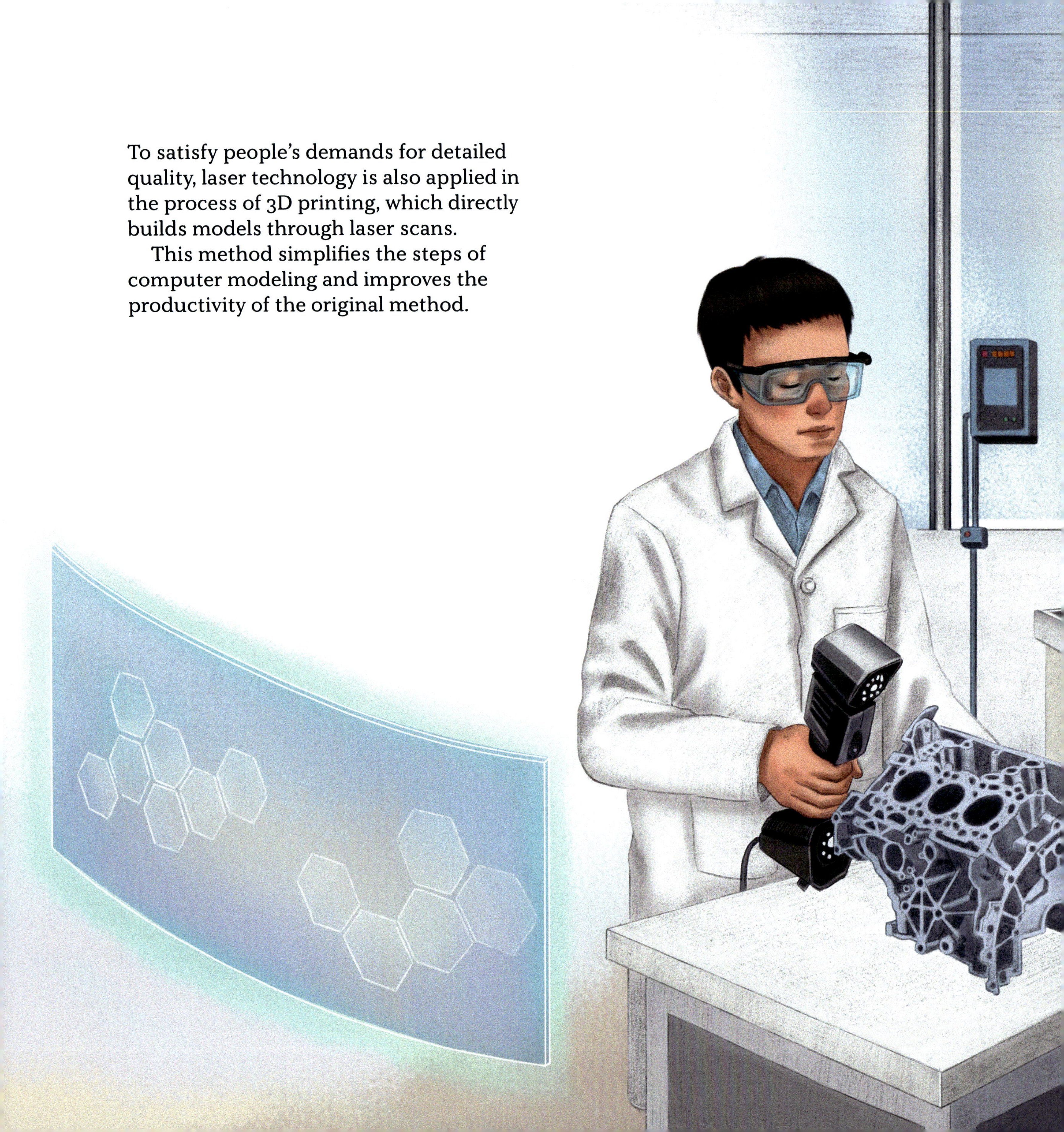

In terms of industrial production, the application of 3D printing technology not only helps meet people's demand for personalization and customization, but also ensures the quality and quantity of products, achieving standardization and personalization simultaneously.

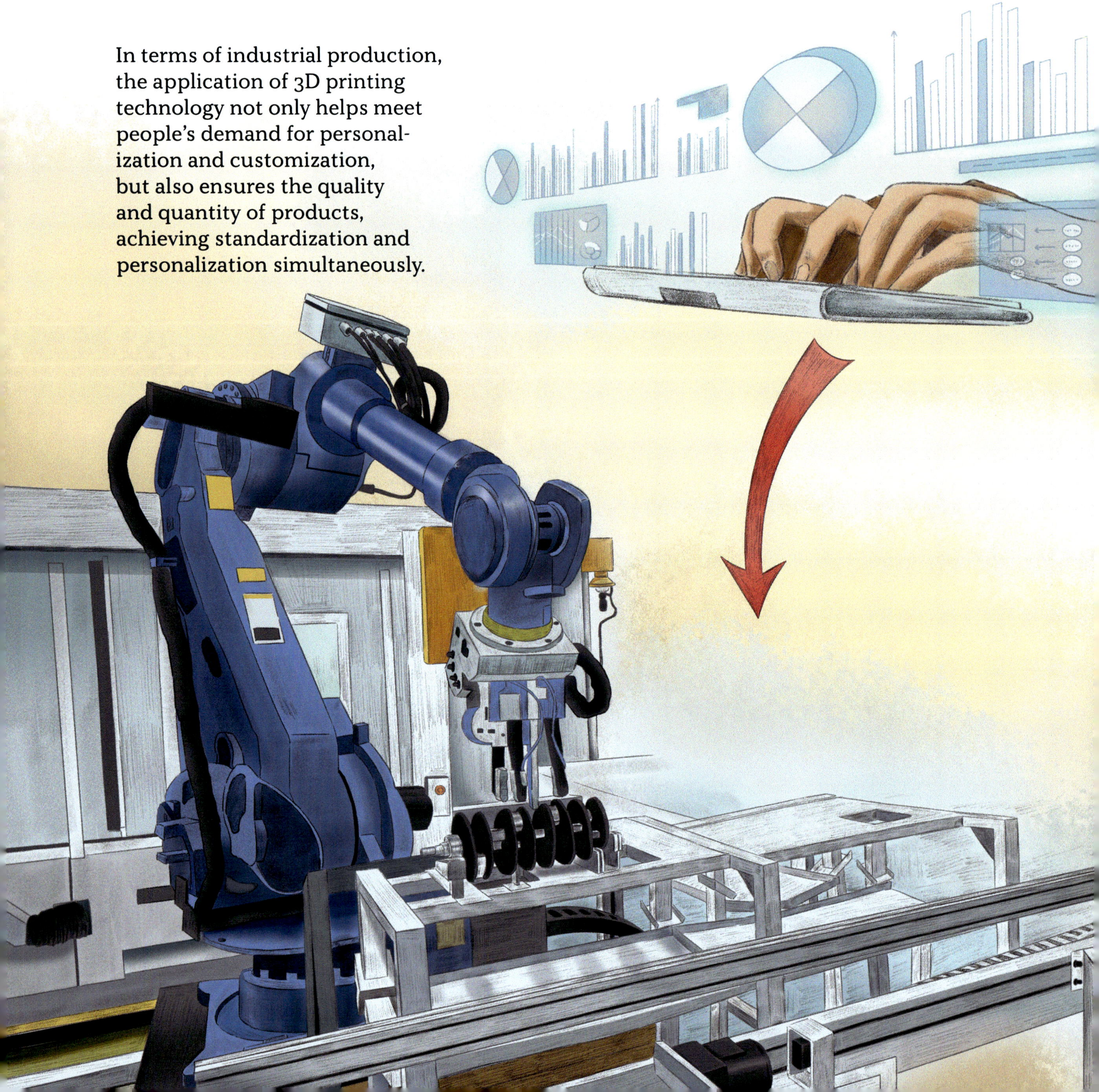

People's pursuit of personalization has gone far beyond the above. Big data and cloud computing have become powerful tools to achieve such pursuits.

By adopting cloud computing, we can collect and analyze big data, predict the trend of consumer activities, and then manufacture products in advance through 3D printing.

Nevertheless, 3D printing highly relies on its materials. Only a limited section of materials are currently available for printing. However, it is promising that more applicable materials will be developed in the near future.

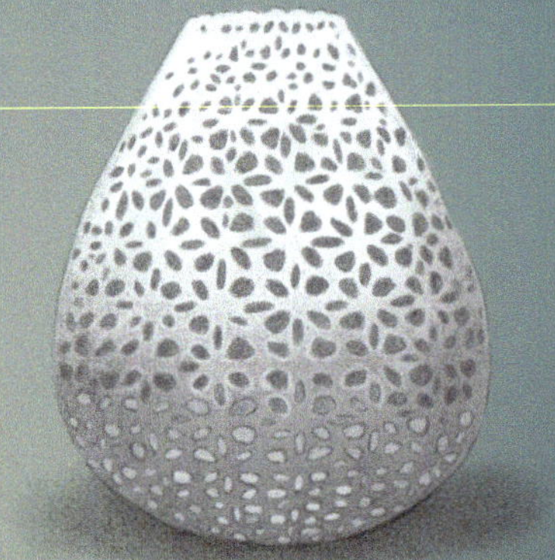

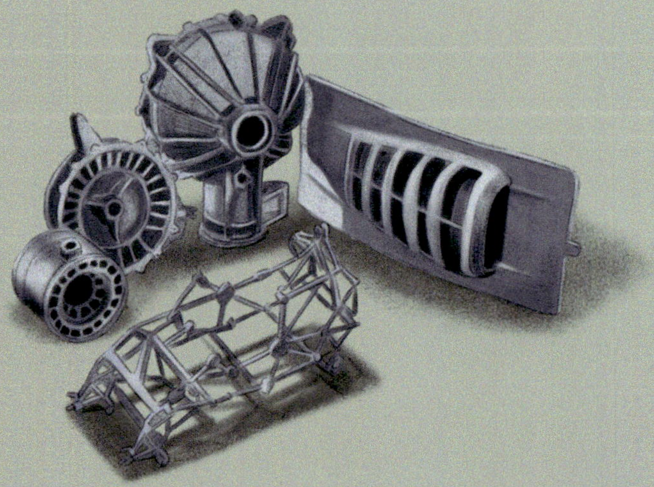

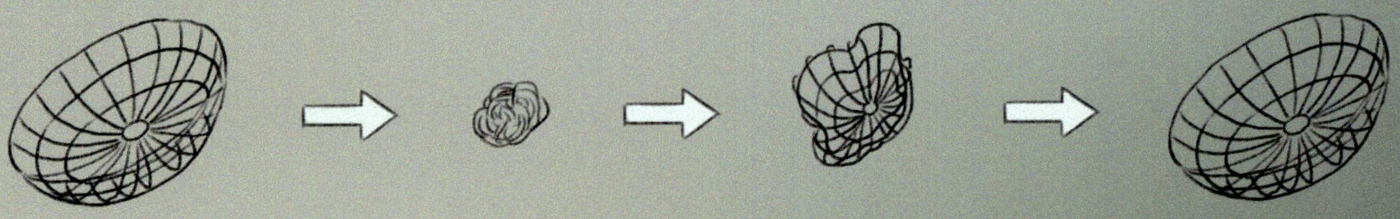

Scientists have also been exploring the 4D printing field recently. The material used for 4D printing technology is a shape memory material that can automatically adapt its form. It will be applied in sectors such as healthcare and underwater vehicles.

Specific applications include underwater detectors, which can automatically bend and transform to form certain shapes based on the varying water temperature in different ocean depths. It can then explore by traveling from broad shallow seas to narrow deep-sea trenches.

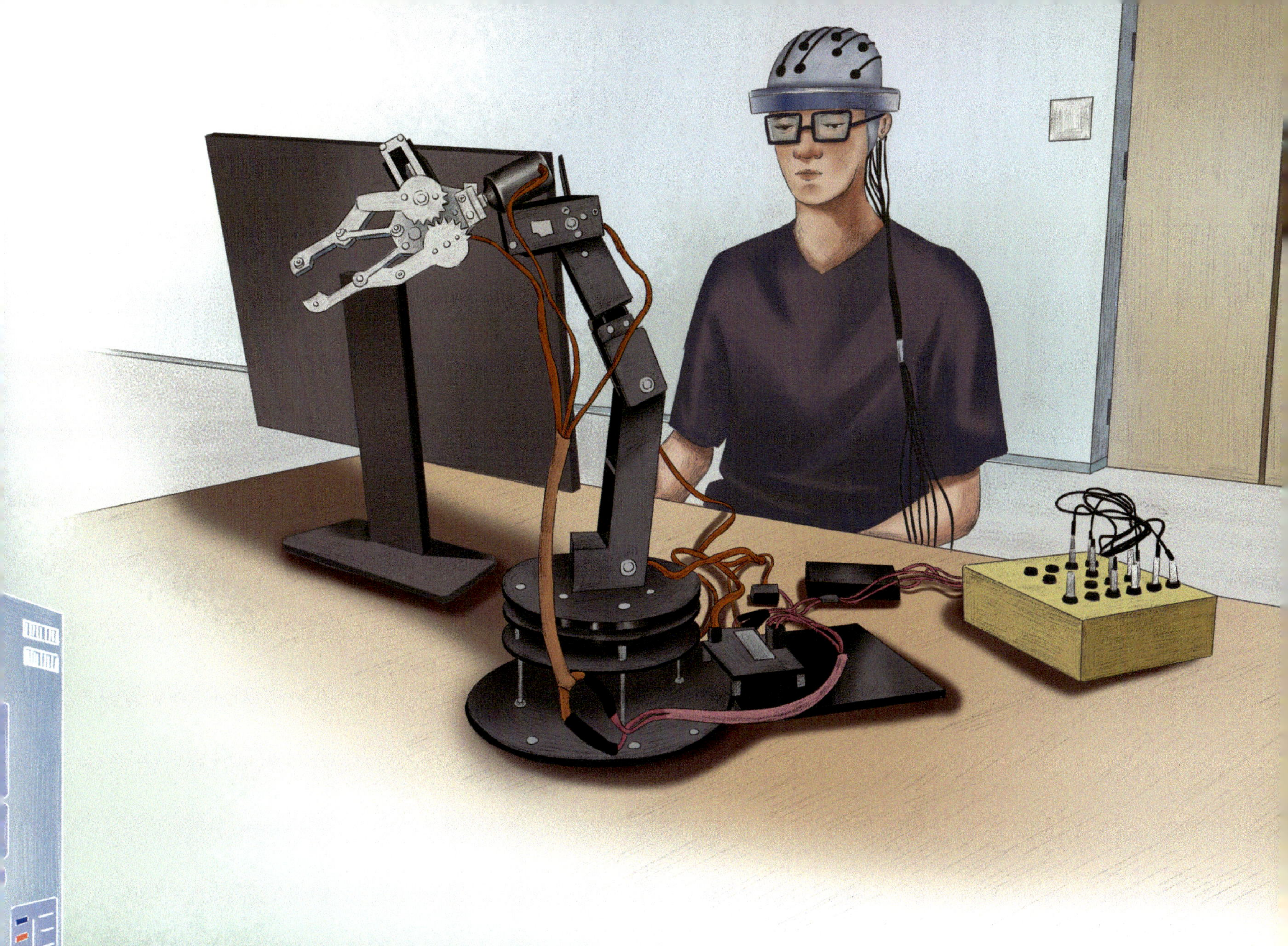

In the future, scientists might combine other technologies with 3D printing, such as nanosensors and brain-machine interfaces. By simply imagining the product we need at home, factories will deliver the final product printed through 3D printing to our home, allowing us to experience "may all your wishes come true."

At present, the 3D printing industry in China is still in the early stages of development.

However, in the aerospace industry, metal 3D printing technology has been widely applied in the production of components of rocket carriers and return capsules. We have even finished the first "Space Printing" mission, which pictures the indefinite possibility for the future construction of space stations.

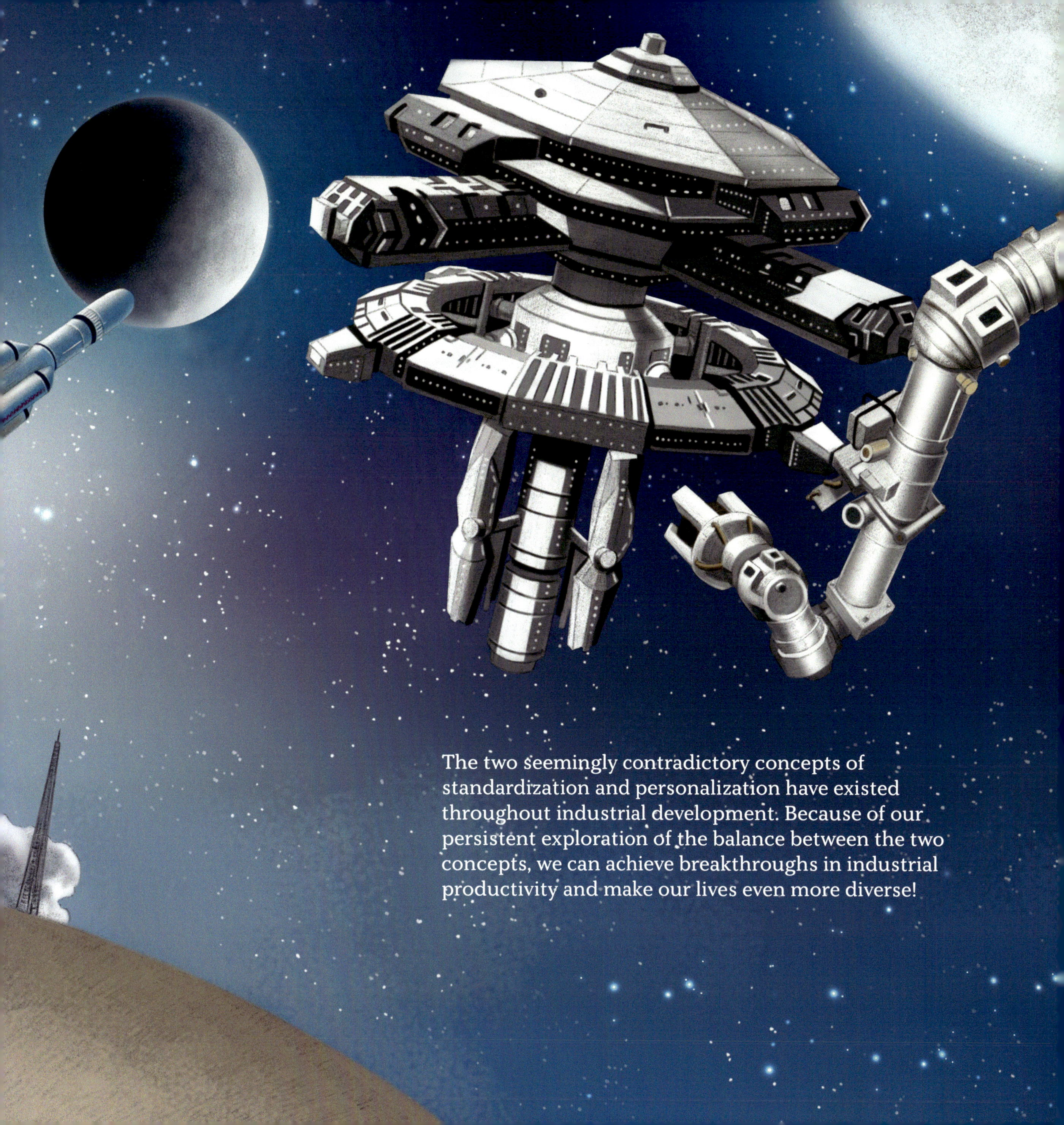

The two seemingly contradictory concepts of standardization and personalization have existed throughout industrial development. Because of our persistent exploration of the balance between the two concepts, we can achieve breakthroughs in industrial productivity and make our lives even more diverse!

Chinese Modern New Technology Series
3D Printing

Edited by Li Chaodong
Translated by Xuemeng Angela Li

First published in 2024 by Royal Collins Publishing Group Inc.
Groupe Publication Royal Collins Inc.
550-555 boul. René-Lévesque O Montréal (Québec) H2Z1B1 Canada

ISBN: 978-1-4878-1236-2

To find out more about our publications, please visit www.royalcollins.com.